wow, the stone age!

In the same collection:

The Flying Pilgrim

wow, the stone age!

[Martin lives in the Upper Paleolithic Era]

victoria bermejo / miguel gallardo

EDICIONES
Aldeasa

Martin opened his eyes. First the left one, then the right, at which point he saw that a deer was gazing steadily at him as if it wished to say something.

The deer came closer and with its mouth began tugging at the goatskin that Martin was wearing, pulling so hard that he pulled it right off and left him with no clothes on, then continued to stare very fixedly. Martin understood from this that the deer wanted to take him somewhere: words are not the only way to make ourselves understood, wouldn't you agree?

Martin looked around to see what his parents were doing.
His mother was at the mouth of the cave carving stones,
as she did every morning. She loved to carve, taking pieces of stone,
striking them against each other, and creating fine tools such as scrapers,
punches, needles, **harpoons** and **engravers**.
Martin's father was fishing in the river.
"Oh dear, fish again", thought Martin, as he preferred to eat meat.

He went up to his mother and said: "Mother, I am going out with this deer", to which his mother replied, "fine, but don't go out in this cold without any clothes on, put on your goatskin and later you can come back here and help me clean the cave, as you know that today we have to throw out the old bones."

The deer looked extremely happy when he saw that Martin was going to following him, going ahead with skips and jumps and moving his horns to indicate how pleased he was.

They went some way until they reached a clearing in the forest where there was the entrance to a cave, at which point the deer made a sign, turning its head as if to say, "come in".

The first room in the cave had a hole like a small window, and Martin looked through in amazement. He saw a group of men doing something he had never seen before.

The men, making use of the rock to create a shape, were carving the outline of an animal on it using an engraving tool. When they had done this, they ground up a piece of burnt coal and used it like a pencil to draw the outline of the animal.

They then took a piece of **iron oxide**, ground it up, mixed it with water and filled in the outlines of the animals, giving them a lovely red colour. Other painted using a brush made of the hair from a **horse's tail**, while others used their fingers or a **leather dabber** which they rubbed against the wall.

Martin had never seen anything like this. Suddenly, all the animals that he knew from real life, in movement, such as **bison**, horses, deer, goats and **aurochs** were there, fixed on the walls, copied by these men. Just as if you had never seen a painting of a car or a house and didn't know that it was possible to do one, then suddenly you came across one. Can you imagine? Wouldn't it be great to discover something for the first time?

When he came out of the cave, excited and happy,
the deer was waiting for him, and Martin, knowing that the deer
could not speak, went up close and gave him a huge hug
to show how grateful he was to the deer for having led him
to the remarkable discovery.
The deer again looked at him in a steady way, as if to say,
did you understand what I was trying to tell you?

Martin went home very impressed
and the first thing he did was to tell his mother,
who was in the kitchen baking the fish.
"Yes, Martin", his mother said. "Those paintings are really marvellous
and if you wish, one day I will show you how to do them".

Martin asked her why they were done, what was the point of them (rather like you asking your mother what advertisements or museums are for) and his mother replied; "well, I think that it is like magic, that they think that the paintings will attract the animals and will make hunting easier...

... but your father thinks that they paint them to represent the male, like you, and the female, like me, so that people can see that there are two sexes in the world. What do you think?" Martin replied, "I think they do it to make something nice, to enjoy looking at the paintings."

However, just in case his mother was right and the paintings were to make the men better hunters, that night Martin got hold of the deer and hid it in his cave, just in case someone was thinking of eating his new friend. And this is exactly what the deer was trying to say with his steady gaze: “save me from the hunters”.

Which is how good friends understand each other just through a look,
and real friendship can save us from every danger.

some words you did not know...

paleolithic
[cover]

the first period of the Stone Age, named after the stones that were used to make implements.

engraver
[p.6]

a tool used to make incisions in stone, bone, horn or wood. This was the tool of the Paleolithic artist, which he used to make the engravings that have survived in caves and on decorated objects.

harpoon
[p.6]

a fishing implement consisting of a long handle and a point which may have one or moor teeth, used for fishing.

iron oxide
[p.12]

a compound resulting from the mixture of oxygen with iron. It has a reddish colour and Paleolithic artists used it to add colour to their paintings.

Horse tail hairs
[p.12]

Paleolithic artists used hairs from horses' tails in the manner of paintbrushes.

Leather dabber
[p.12]

small bundle of rags or skins used to add volume to the painted figures.

bison
[p.14]

an animal similar to a bull with very heavy rear quarters covered in rough hair and with short horns. Found throughout Europe in the Paleolithic era.

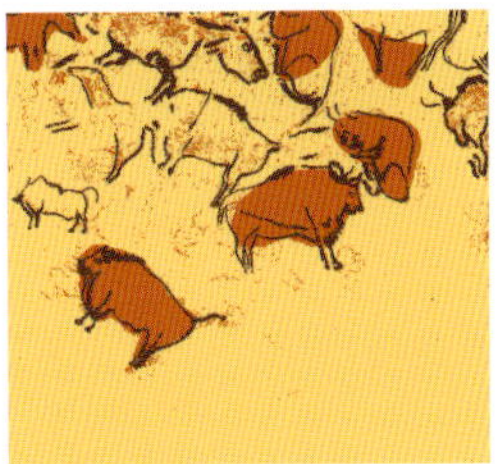

aurochs
[p.14]

also similar to a bull, but larger, and very common in central Europe, but which became extinct in 1627.

Coordination and production: Ediciones Aldeasa

Written by: Victoria Bermejo

Illustrated by: Miguel Gallardo

Translated by: Laura Suffield

Graphic Design: Carmen Olivares

Layout: Marie Genevieve

Repro: Cromotex

Printed by: Artes gráficas Palermo, S.L.

ISBN: 84-8003-910-8

Depósito Legal: M-18331-2004

wow, the stone age!